T0210189

# Three Tales of Deadly Desire

## Pamela Pollack and Meg Belviso

Series Editors:
Rob Waring and Sue Leather
Series Story Consultant: Julian Thomlinson
Story Editor: Sue Leather

NATIONAL
GEOGRAPHIC
LEARNING

CENGAGE
Learning·

Australia • Brazil • Japan • Korea • Mexico • Singapore • Spain • United Kingdom • United States

Page Turners Reading Library

**Three Tales of Deadly Desire**

Pamela Pollack and Meg Belviso

**Publisher:** Andrew Robinson

**Executive Editor:** Sean Bermingham

**Development Editor:**
Charlotte Sharman

**Associate Development Editor:**
Sarah Tan

**Editorial Assistant:** Vivian Chua

**Director of Global Marketing:**
Ian Martin

**Senior Content Project Manager:**
Tan Jin Hock

**Manufacturing Planner:**
Mary Beth Hennebury

**Contributor:** Jessie Chew

**Layout Design and Illustrations:**
Redbean Design Pte Ltd

**Cover Illustration:** Eric Foenander

ISBN-13: 978-1-4240-4654-6

ISBN-10: 1-4240-4654-8

**National Geographic Learning**
20 Channel Center Street
Boston, Massachusetts 02210
USA

Cengage Learning is a leading provider of customized learning solutions with office locations around the globe, including Singapore, the United Kingdom, Australia, Mexico, Brazil, and Japan. Locate your local office at:
**international.cengage.com/region**

Cengage Learning products are represented in Canada by Nelson Education, Ltd.

Visit National Geographic Learning online at
**NGL.Cengage.com**

Visit our corporate website at
**www.cengage.com**

Printed in the United States of America
2 3 4 5 6 7 – 17 16

# Contents

## Review

## Background Reading

# The Perfect Wife
## People in the story

**Greg Bulstrow**
a songwriter in his mid-30s

**Missy Bulstrow**
Greg's wife, a sweet and
pretty woman in her mid-20s

**Mrs. Root**
the elderly owner of a shop
that sells many different things

This story is set in the USA.

# Chapter 1

# What good are love songs?

Greg Bulstrow knew all about love. He wrote love songs that were played on the radio all the time. His songs made him a lot of money so he had almost everything he wanted, but as he walked down the street with his guitar, he felt alone. His girlfriend had just left him. He thought she was his true love and imagined that they would be together forever, but they fought all the time and didn't make each other happy. That morning she'd walked out, leaving him alone.

That wasn't love, Greg said to himself. He turned the corner onto a dark, quiet street that he didn't know. People in love should never fight. A woman should love a man more than anything. She should care about him more than herself. *Why can't I find a woman like that?* Greg was so angry that he wanted to throw his guitar away. After all, what good were love songs if you didn't have love?

Greg dreamed about his perfect love for a long time. He knew just what she would look like. She would have dark hair and dark eyes, and she would look at him as if he were the only person in the world. He saw her in his dreams and he wrote all his songs about her, but he could never find her in the real world.

It started to rain. Greg ran to the open door of a store. Above the door was a sign that read "MRS. ROOT HAS WHAT YOU WANT." *No store could have what I want*, Greg thought. But he went inside.

The store was small with many shelves filled with strange things. There were little bottles and jars, old rings, painted toys, a monkey made of gold. It made Greg think of magic. Behind the counter was a woman so small she almost couldn't see over the counter. She had white hair piled up on her head. Greg thought this must be Mrs. Root who owned the store.

"Trouble in love?" Mrs. Root asked.

"How did you know that?" Greg said.

"I see it on your face," said Mrs. Root. "You want to find the perfect woman."

"That's not possible," said Greg. He put his guitar down on the counter. "I write a lot of love songs, but there's no love in my life."

"I could find you the woman of your dreams," she said.

"How could you do that?" Greg asked.

"It's my secret," said Mrs. Root. "But I can do it. For a price."

"What kind of price?"

Mrs. Root laid her hand on Greg's guitar. "If you give me your music, I'll give you the girl you want."

"Give you my music?" Greg said with a laugh. "If you want to listen to my songs you can buy them just like millions of other people. Or hear them for free on the radio."

"I don't want to listen to your songs," she said. "I want the part of you that creates them. It's worth more than you know."

Greg wasn't sure if Mrs. Root was joking. "How can you take that from me?" he said. "It's part of who I am. That would be like . . ."

"Like magic?" Mrs. Root said. "Something like that. You give me the part of you that is able to write songs. I give you the girl of your dreams."

"So I wouldn't be able to write songs anymore?" Greg said. "I don't believe you."

"That's my price, believe it or not," Mrs. Root said. "If you say yes, you'll never write another song but you'll have the love you dream about. Do you want to sing about love or have it?"

Something about Mrs. Root made Greg believe her. He had so many hit songs that he didn't need to sell any more. But he didn't have the woman of his dreams. Why not take a chance? "What good are love songs if you don't have love?" he said. "It's a deal."

Mrs. Root nodded and took Greg's guitar. Outside, the rain stopped, and Greg turned to go. As he was leaving, Mrs. Root gave Greg a little bride and groom. "Go home," she said. "Your wife is waiting."

Greg still wasn't sure he believed Mrs. Root. Could she really bring him a woman he only dreamed about? He had to get home to find out.

When Greg got home he thought he heard someone in his kitchen. "Hello?" he called. "Is someone there?"

A beautiful woman with dark hair and dark eyes came out to him. She looked at Greg as if he were the only person in the world.

Greg couldn't believe it. Was he dreaming? He closed and opened his eyes. The woman was still there.

"Welcome home, my love," she said. "I've been waiting for you."

# Chapter 2

# Not like a real woman

The woman called Missy was everything Greg wanted in a woman. She sang all his songs to him, and they never fought. Missy liked everything Greg liked and she loved him more than anything.

Greg and Missy got married. He never thought about his lost guitar. Now that he had the girl of his dreams, he didn't need to write love songs.

One day they went out to work in the garden. Greg wanted a garden but he didn't have the time to plant flowers. Missy had time to plant flowers. She asked Greg which he liked best and planted his favorites.

"I love lilies," Missy said, planting a white, sweet one next to some roses.

"Lilies are my favorite flowers," said Greg.

"That's why I love them," Missy said, touching the dirt around the lily. "I love all the flowers that make you happy."

Greg didn't know how he'd lived without her. He picked a lily and handed it to Missy. "For you, my love," he said.

Missy also picked a lily and handed it to Greg. "I don't want to have anything if you don't have one too," she said.

Greg kissed Missy for always thinking of him before she thought of herself.

Since Greg didn't write music anymore, he spent all his time with Missy. They went to the beach, ate dinner together, and listened to music. He never wanted to be anywhere but at her side.

One day a song came on the radio that Greg thought was silly. "What do you think of this song?" he asked Missy.

"I don't like it," she said. "I think it's silly. Your songs are much better."

Greg liked the way Missy understood music. A few days later, one of his favorite songs came on the radio. "What do you think of this song?" he asked Missy.

"It's my favorite," she said.

Greg was surprised they had the same favorite song. Missy really was his perfect wife. The next day he asked Missy what she liked best about him. He imagined what he thought the perfect wife would say. *She would say that she loves everything about me*, he thought.

"What's your favorite thing about me?" he asked Missy.

"I love everything about you," she said.

For the first time Greg didn't feel happy when Missy said the right thing. He wished Missy could surprise him. It was as if she was a girl in one of his love songs who only said what he wanted her to say. Somehow she was not like a real woman, so even when he was with her he felt alone. *How can I feel alone when someone loves me so much?* Greg thought.

Greg took out some paper. Whenever he was sad he usually wrote a song about it to make himself feel better. But now he couldn't think of any words. Then he remembered giving Mrs. Root his music. He would never write another song again.

*That's impossible,* Greg thought. *I've always been able to write songs before. I just haven't tried in a long time.*

Greg became afraid. How could his music really be gone? Could he never get it back?

Missy came into the room and kissed him. "What are you doing, my love?" she asked.

"I was trying to write a song," Greg said. "I can't."

Missy touched his head. "You don't need to write songs any more," she said. "You have me now. I'm all you need and I'll never leave you."

# Chapter 3

# Unusual plant

"Tell me something you like other than me," Greg asked Missy one day over breakfast.

"I like music and lilies and your love songs," she said.

"Those are things I like too," said Greg. "There must be some things you like that I don't. Do you like horses, for example?" he asked.

"I don't know," said Missy. "Do you?"

"I don't know anything about horses," said Greg.

"Then neither do I," said Missy. "I don't know if I like them."

"It shouldn't matter what I think about them," Greg said.

Missy frowned. "I don't understand," she said. "How can I like something if you don't like it? I'm your wife."

"Wives don't have to agree with their husbands all the time," Greg said.

"Yes, they do," said Missy. "If I like things that you don't, we could fight. People in love should never fight."

Greg used to believe the same thing. Now he wasn't so sure. He wished Missy would think of herself instead of him sometimes. But even though he tried hard, he couldn't change Missy. She always said he was right about everything. She said he was handsome and smart and the best man in the world and she made his favorite breakfast every morning.

The more Missy loved Greg the less Greg loved Missy. When he tried to go for a walk by himself, Missy ran after him. She didn't want to be without him even for a minute.

One night when Missy was sleeping, Greg went to the kitchen where the bride and groom Mrs. Root gave him sat on the table. Greg took out some paper to write a song. It was the only way he could talk about how unhappy he was. He sat at the table for hours. The sun came up and the paper was still empty.

Missy came into the kitchen to make him breakfast. "I missed you," she said. "You didn't kiss me when I woke up." Then she added, "I want to spend all day together today."

"I have to go see someone alone," Greg said.

Missy looked sad. "What will I do while you're gone?" she asked.

"Why don't you go to the flower show in town?" Greg said. "You like flowers."

Greg went to see Mrs. Root to see if she could give him back his music and send Missy away. When he got to her store Mrs. Root was watering a tall green plant with orange fruit. She didn't look surprised to see him. "Trouble in love?" she asked again.

"I want my music back," Greg said. He could see his guitar hanging on the wall behind the gold monkey. "I can't live without writing songs anymore."

"What about Missy?" Mrs. Root asked. "Your perfect wife. I made her just for you."

"I don't want to be married to Missy anymore," Greg said. "I thought she was what I wanted but I've never been so unhappy. Can you give me back my music and take her away?"

"A deal is a deal, forever," Mrs. Root said. "It's just like when you get married. Until you die."

Greg let his head fall on the counter. "Then I'm going to be unhappy the rest of my life," he said.

Greg watched Mrs. Root cut at the leaves of the plant. Greg didn't know the fruit but it smelled so sweet it made him forget about Missy for a moment. "What kind of plant is that?" he asked her.

"A very unusual plant," she said. "The fruit is sweet but very dangerous. Anyone who eats it will die."

Greg thought about Missy, who loved sweet things just like he did. He wished she would eat the fruit and die. Then he would be free. *Maybe if Missy was dead I would get my music back*, Greg thought.

"How much for a piece of that fruit?" Greg asked.

Mrs. Root picked one off the plant. "I'll give you one for free," she said.

Greg took the fruit home.

# Chapter 4

# A piece of cake

Greg didn't want to live with Missy anymore, but could he kill her?

"I missed you while you were gone today." Missy kissed him as he came in. This was just what he always wanted from his wife, but Greg couldn't wait to get away from Missy.

She took Greg's coat.

"I didn't want to go to the flower show without you," Missy said. "We can go together tomorrow."

"I don't want to go," he said.

"If you don't want to go, I don't want to go either," Missy said. "It's not fun without you. I don't want to fight."

Greg's head started to hurt. He was angry at Missy, but she was just trying to make him happy. "What did you do while I was gone if you didn't go to the flower show?" he asked.

"I thought about what to make for your dinner," Missy said. "Then I waited for you." Missy hung up Greg's coat.

Greg thought of Missy sitting at the kitchen table all day, waiting for him to come home. Sitting for hours by the little bride and groom. If Greg wasn't with her, Missy didn't know what to do. How could Greg ever go out by himself if he knew Missy needed him that much?

"Greg?" Missy asked. "What's this?"

She put her hand in his coat pocket and pulled out the orange fruit. "I've never seen this kind of fruit before," she said. "Do you like it? I want to know all the fruits you like. I can take this fruit and make something special just for you."

Greg could not live with Missy another minute.

"I brought the fruit for you, my love," he said. "It's a very special fruit. The sweetest you've ever tasted. It's all for you."

"You're wonderful," said Missy.

Greg lay down before dinner. He thought he should take the fruit away from Missy before she ate it, but if he took it away, he would never be free of her. If he wanted his music, Missy had to die.

Greg sat down for one last dinner with Missy. "This is a wonderful meal, my love," he said. Missy would not be alive much longer. Greg could be nice to her until then.

"Wait until you see the dessert," said Missy. "I made it just for you." Then Missy brought a large cake from the kitchen. She cut a big piece for Greg and one for herself. "I hope you like it," she said.

"I'm sure I'll love it," Greg said. Missy looked very pretty at the table. Greg remembered one of his old love songs about the girl with dark hair who looked at him like he was the only man in the world. He still loved the song. He sang it to himself as he ate his cake. "Did you like the fruit I gave you?" he asked.

"It tastes great," said Missy. "Do you like it?"

"What do you mean, do I like it?" Greg asked. "I gave the fruit to you." Suddenly Greg felt a terrible pain. It felt like he had eaten something awful.

"I could never keep such a sweet piece of fruit all for myself," Missy said. "I put it into the cake so that we could share it. It's the sweetest thing I've ever tasted."

Greg fell forward onto the table. He should have guessed. Missy didn't know the fruit would kill him. But she never wanted to have anything if he couldn't have it too. He and Missy would be together now. Forever.

The last thing Greg saw before his eyes closed in death was the little bride and groom on the table.

# The Golden Monkey
## People in the story

**Benny Platt**
a man in his late 20s, who
lies and steals

**Deb**
Benny's previous girlfriend

**Joe**
Benny's friend who likes
bowling

**Mrs. Root**
the elderly owner of a shop
that sells many different things

This story is set in the USA.

# Chapter 1

# Something for nothing

Benny Platt looked at all the things for sale in Mrs. Root's store: jewelry, strange objects, little bottles—even a guitar hanging on the wall. Benny wanted a lot of things in there, but he didn't have the money to buy any of them. He never had enough money and it wasn't fair, he thought. No matter what he did he never got rich. Other men had important jobs that paid a lot of money and got everything they wanted but Benny had nothing.

Mrs. Root stood behind the counter. "Anything here can be yours if you can pay the price," she said.

Benny couldn't pay for most of the things in the store, so he turned to leave the store. But then he saw something on the shelf next to the door. It was a monkey made of gold. Benny loved gold. He went over to the monkey. There was a sign in front that read: I BRING WHATEVER YOU DESIRE.

"I wish I could have whatever I desired," Benny said. He touched the monkey's head. "I never get anything I want."

Mrs. Root appeared beside him and took Benny's hand off the statue. "You can't pay for this," she said. "It costs far too much for you."

Benny looked at little Mrs. Root with her white hair piled up on her head. How did she know he couldn't pay for the monkey? Could she tell that nothing in Benny's life ever worked out the way he planned? He had lost every job he ever had and he wasn't lucky in other ways. Even his girlfriend, Deb, left him. Now Mrs. Root was telling him he couldn't even afford a gold monkey.

"How much do you want for it?" he said angrily. "Whatever you want, I'll pay for it." Benny didn't know how he would get the money but he didn't want Mrs. Root to know that.

Mrs. Root smiled. "The price of the monkey is everything you have. Will you pay that price?"

Benny laughed. "No," he said. "You must think I'm stupid. You can keep your monkey."

"That's a smart choice," Mrs. Root said. "Believe me, you don't want this monkey."

Benny went out onto the street. He felt the monkey's jeweled eyes watching him from inside the store. But Benny knew something that Mrs. Root didn't know. When Benny wanted something he knew how to get it without anyone even knowing. He was a thief. He was going to get the monkey without paying for it, he decided.

That night after midnight, Benny came back to Mrs. Root's dark, empty store. He knew how to open doors without using a key, and this one opened easily. Benny stepped inside and went to the shelf where the golden monkey sat. But it wasn't there.

Benny looked around the dark store. He saw a flash of gold on the counter. The monkey sat right in front of Benny, almost as if Mrs. Root had left it out for him to find. Its jeweled eyes sparkled. "You're mine now," Benny said out loud. He tucked the monkey into his jacket and left the store, closing the door behind him.

Mrs. Root said the monkey would cost everything that Benny had. Instead he had it for free. He had what he wanted and she couldn't stop him.

Benny brought the monkey back to his apartment and put it on the table next to his bed. He remembered the sign that was in front of the monkey at Mrs. Root's store: I BRING WHATEVER YOU DESIRE.

Benny didn't believe in magic but before he went to sleep he touched the monkey on the head. "I want eggs tomorrow morning," he said. "Let's see if you can do that."

Benny fell asleep feeling happy.

# Chapter 2

# Anything you desire

The next morning Benny woke to the smell of eggs coming from his own kitchen. There was a plate waiting for him on the kitchen table. The golden monkey sat beside it.

Benny stared at the plate. How could this be? Benny tasted the eggs. They were cooked just the way he liked them. The monkey knew exactly what he wanted.

Benny thought he should test the monkey again. "I want a new jacket," he said. "The one I saw in the window of the store in town." Benny waited. Nothing happened. Then he went into the bedroom and found a new jacket lying on the bed with the monkey on the table beside it. *This really works,* Benny told himself as he put on the jacket. *The monkey will bring me anything I want.*

Benny thought of a lot of other things he wanted and everything he asked for appeared in his apartment. Very soon he had new clothes, a new television and games, his favorite dessert. Mrs. Root didn't give him what he wanted and Benny stole the best thing in her store! Now there was nothing he couldn't have.

*I have to show Deb*, Benny thought. Deb had said she didn't want to see Benny anymore. But that was before Benny got lucky. Now, thanks to his monkey, he could give Deb anything she wanted.

Benny left the apartment and walked to where his old car was parked. *Why didn't I ask for a new car?* he asked himself

as he walked. *A red sports car.* Benny turned the corner. There, in the place where he had parked his old car, was a red sports car waiting for him. The golden monkey sat in the front seat. Benny didn't ask for the car, but it was there. The monkey brought it to him anyway just because he thought it. Benny asked the monkey for a gold necklace to give to Deb.

Benny drove to Deb's house. Now that he could give her anything she wanted, she would want to be with him, Benny was sure. "Things have changed," Benny told Deb, giving her the necklace when she answered the door. "Please come back to me."

Deb pushed the necklace away. "How did you get this necklace and your new clothes and your new car sitting outside?" she asked. "You stole them, didn't you?"

"No!" Benny said. "Someone gave them to me." That was almost true. The monkey gave Benny everything. Benny only stole the monkey. "Is there someone else?" he asked. "Do you love another man? Someone richer than me?"

"No, Benny," said Deb, "there is no other man. When I met you, you had a job. You didn't make much money but at least you weren't a thief. I left you because you became one. I don't care if you buy me jewelry or drive an expensive car. You just have to learn that you can't get something for nothing."

Benny didn't understand. "But I can give you whatever you want," Benny said. "Why does it matter where it comes from? You must love a man who can give you everything."

"I can't love a thief," said Deb. "I never will."

*Oh, yes you will*, Benny thought. *Even if my monkey has to make you love me.*

Benny left Deb's house and got into his new car. The monkey sat on the seat beside him. Benny didn't have Deb yet, but he had everything else.

# Chapter 3

# The best thing that ever happened to me

Benny liked bowling and went often. One night his friend Joe asked him to go bowling. Benny's new ball was better than everyone else's bowling balls. Benny never won a game before, but tonight he knew he would beat everyone just because he wanted to win.

All night Benny played well, while the other players dropped their balls and fell down. Benny won the game easily. "That was great," Joe said when the game was over. "You're the best!"

Benny got into his car and put his bowling prize on the seat next to him. He thought he should be happy but he wasn't. Everyone else played so badly that Benny didn't feel like he had won the game. He felt like he stole the prize. The monkey made Benny win, but it couldn't make Benny feel like a winner.

Benny stopped bowling. It wasn't fun anymore. He sat in his apartment. The monkey brought him more new clothes and games before Benny even asked for them. But it didn't make Benny happy. In fact, he almost wished he never took the monkey.

The next afternoon Benny lay on his bed looking at his bowling prize. He remembered when he was a little boy he won first place in a running race. Benny ran faster than everyone else that day. It made the young Benny feel good because he won it himself; there was no golden monkey

making the other runners slow. Benny really won. He felt great that day, like a winner. He hadn't felt that good in a long time.

Benny rolled over on his bed. There on the table next to the bowling prize was Benny's prize for running the fastest that day. He cried out and sat up, staring at what the monkey had brought. The monkey knew that Benny wanted it, but holding the prize in his hands didn't make him happy. Not like when he won it all by himself. As long as the monkey helped him get things, Benny would never feel that he won them himself.

Benny left his apartment to get away from the monkey. He went to a park and sat down. There was a woman running, children playing, a man walking his dog. They all looked happy.

A man and a woman walked past Benny holding hands. They made Benny think of Deb. The woman looked up at the man. "You're the best thing that's ever happened to me," she said. How Benny wished Deb would look at him that way and say that to him.

A few minutes later someone sat beside Benny. He looked around and saw it was Deb. "You're the best thing that's ever happened to me, Benny," she said.

Benny was happier than ever before. Finally he had Deb's love. "Things will be different now," Benny promised. "I'll make you happy and I won't steal anymore."

"You make me happy just the way you are," said Deb. "I will still love you if you're a thief. You're the best thing that ever happened to me."

Benny went cold. He realized that Deb wasn't saying these things because she really loved him. The monkey was making her say what Benny wanted to hear. It was just like with his prizes. Benny didn't really have Deb's love, so it couldn't make him happy. Deb would only love Benny if the monkey made her love him. But as long as the monkey was making her love him, Benny could never believe it was really love.

Benny jumped up and ran home. The monkey was waiting on the table. He picked it up, jumped into his car, and drove to the river. He walked out beside the water and threw the monkey into the river. It fell into the water and it was gone.

Benny drove home. He threw himself on his bed, happy the monkey was no longer there. He didn't need it to bring him things anymore. All he needed was a hot cup of coffee.

When Benny got to the kitchen he smelled coffee. There was a hot cup of coffee on the table. Beside the coffee sat the golden monkey.

# Chapter 4

# Final wish

Benny ran outside, jumped into his car, and drove as fast as he could to Mrs. Root's store. When he got there she was closing up for the night. "I need to see you!" Benny said as he ran through the door.

"Hello Mr. Platt," said Mrs. Root. She touched her white hair. "Did you come back to steal something else?"

"I'm sorry I stole from you," Benny said.

"I'm sure you are," said Mrs. Root.

"I took the golden monkey," Benny said. "I'm sorry. I want to give it back."

Mrs. Root smiled. "I can't take the monkey back," she said. "The monkey knows who its owner is."

"But I don't want it!" said Benny.

"Why did you take it if you didn't want it?" Mrs. Root said. "I told you the monkey cost far too much for you. But you took it anyway."

Benny put his face in his hands. "Isn't there any way I can be free of it?" he asked Mrs. Root.

"The monkey gives you whatever you desire," Mrs. Root said. "When you have no more desires the monkey will leave you."

Benny left the store. As long as he desired anything the monkey would be his. But how could he stop wanting things?

For as long as he could remember, Benny wanted things. Could he ever stop?

Benny thought of Deb. She didn't want any of the things Benny tried to give her. She knew how to be happy with what she had and never understood why Benny wanted so much. Benny needed to talk to her.

When he got home the monkey was waiting with the phone. Benny called her number and Deb answered.

"I need to talk to you," he said.

"You can tell me anything, Benny," said Deb. "You're the best thing that ever happened to me."

Benny wished that Deb was telling the truth but he knew she wasn't. "Please," said Benny. "All those things you said to me about being a thief. You were right. I know that now. But I don't know how to change. You have to help me."

"How can I help you, Benny?" asked Deb.

"I need you to tell me the truth," Benny said. "That necklace I wanted to give you. It was beautiful but you didn't want it. Why not?"

"I don't care about jewels," Deb said. "I cared about you. I wanted you to be a better man."

Benny hung up the phone. He knew Deb was telling the truth. She wanted him to be a better man. What could be better than getting her everything she wanted, no matter what the price? *There must be another man!* Benny thought. *A man better than me.* Benny was sure Deb was with someone else. Someone with even more money than Benny. He might have been there with Deb when Benny called. Benny felt terrible that Deb was happy with someone else. It wasn't fair. Benny didn't want her to be happy with anyone else!

He only wanted her to be with him. If he couldn't have Deb, Benny wished that nobody else could have her either. He wished . . .

"Deb? Deb!" Benny picked up the phone again, but Deb was already gone.

The Golden Monkey had disappeared from the table beside the phone.

"No!" Benny cried. But it was too late. He made a wish, even if he didn't say it out loud. "Deb!"

Benny ran to his car. He drove across town to Deb's house. He ran to the front door. It was open. Deb lay on the living room floor. She was dead. Beside her sat the golden monkey. Its jeweled eyes seemed to look at Benny.

Deb was dead. The monkey had granted Benny's wish. Now no one else could have her. He sat beside her on the floor. Deb was gone forever. The monkey was here to stay. Benny would never be rid of it. Not for the rest of his life. *I wish I was dead*, Benny thought.

The last thing Benny saw was the monkey's jeweled eyes as it gave him his final wish.

# Beauty Secret
## People in the story

**Lena Howe**
a beautiful woman in her
early 40s, who is afraid of
getting old

**Rand Howe**
Lena's handsome husband

**Lizbeth**
Lena's friend at the gym,
also in her early 40s

**Mrs. Root**
the elderly owner of a shop
that sells many different things

This story is set in the USA.

# Chapter 1

# Anything to be young again

Lena Howe worked out very hard in her gym class but when she looked in the mirror in the dressing room she thought she looked old. Old was ugly, and Lena had always been beautiful. She couldn't face being ugly.

Her cell phone rang. It was her husband, Rand. "I'm coming home late tonight," he said. "I have work to do at the office."

This was the fourth time this week Rand would be late home. Maybe he didn't want to see her, Lena thought. Maybe he was with a younger woman. Lena tried special foods, exercise, and clothes to look young but nothing worked.

Lena's friend Lizbeth came into the dressing room. Lena hadn't seen her in a few weeks, and Lizbeth looked beautiful. "How do you do it?" Lena asked.

"It's a beauty secret," Lizbeth said.

Lena frowned. "What kind of secret? Can I buy it in a store?"

"It costs a lot," said Lizbeth. "It's very hard to get."

"I don't care," said Lena. "I need to have it." Lizbeth turned away. Lena did not think she wanted to help her. "I thought we were friends," she said. "Why won't you share it with me?"

"All right," Lizbeth said. "If you really want it that badly, you have to go see Mrs. Root at her shop. It's her secret so it's up to her to tell you."

Lena left the gym and drove to the store on the other side of the city. The street was dark and the store was small, but Lena couldn't wait to meet the woman who made Lizbeth look so young.

Mrs. Root was behind the counter. She had white hair piled up on her head. "Have you come for my special beauty bath?" Mrs. Root asked.

"How did you know that?" said Lena. Did Lizbeth tell Mrs. Root she was coming?

"I know the face of a woman who's lost her love," Mrs. Root said. "Come with me."

Mrs. Root led Lena to a room in the back of the store full of bowls on shelves. Mrs. Root put plants into a bowl and mixed them up. "This is the secret ingredient," Mrs. Root said picking up a red bottle. "It won't work without it."

She mixed it all together and gave Lena a bottle with the beauty bath in it. "Soak in this for one hour," she said. "You'll be beautiful again."

"How much is it?" Lena asked.

"Try it," said Mrs. Root. "When you see how it works, you'll know how much to pay."

Lena took the bottle home. Rand was working late. Lena filled the bathtub with water and put in the special beauty bath.

The water in the bathtub turned red and thick. Lena didn't want to sit in it. Then she remembered Rand didn't kiss her goodbye that morning. What if this was her only chance to be beautiful to him again? She had to try anything.

Lena stepped into the bathtub and sat down in the red water. "I'd do anything to be young again," she said. "Anything."

The next morning Lena made breakfast for Rand. Usually in the morning Rand read a newspaper and didn't talk to Lena. This morning he didn't open the paper. "You look different," he said.

Could the beauty bath be working, Lena wondered? Rand didn't stop looking at her. When it was time for him to leave for work, he didn't want to go.

"It's OK if I'm a little late today," Rand said. "Why don't we go for a walk? Just the two of us?"

Lena and Rand took a walk in the park. They held hands. Rand never stopped looking at Lena. When they got home she looked in the mirror. She looked young again.

All week Rand came home early. He brought Lena flowers and took her dancing. Then, suddenly things changed. One morning when Lena got up, Rand was reading the newspaper. He didn't kiss her goodbye or come home for dinner. He said he had too much work to do.

Lena looked in the mirror. She looked older again. Mrs. Root's special bath wasn't working anymore. Lena needed to get more beauty bath fast.

## Chapter 2

# Secret ingredient

Lena visited Mrs. Root the next day for her beauty bath. When Lena came into the store Mrs. Root led her into the back room. The plants for the bath were on the table but they weren't cut. "You haven't paid for your bath yet," Mrs. Root said.

"I have money," said Lena.

"I don't need money," said Mrs. Root, pointing to the plants on the table. "It's hard doing all the work myself. I need someone I can teach to be like me. I think you're the right woman."

"I don't know anything about plants or working in a store," Lena said.

"I'll teach you everything you need to know," said Mrs. Root. "In return for your help, I'll give you your bath."

Lena looked around the store at the shelves full of strange things, old jewelry, a guitar, even a monkey made of gold. It was nothing like the stores where Lena shopped with her friends. Lena never wanted to work in a store like this. But if Mrs. Root could make her beautiful, maybe Rand would take her dancing that night.

"I'll help you," she said.

Mrs. Root showed Lena how to cut the plants for her bath and taught her which plants to use. Lena mixed the leaves in a bowl. Mrs. Root gave Lena a red bottle full of the special ingredient.

Lena put the ingredient in the bottle into the bowl and mixed it all together. "What is the special ingredient?" Lena asked.

"You'll find that out when the time is right," Mrs. Root said. "You have a lot to learn."

Lena visited Mrs. Root more and more. She taught her about the things in her store such as the guitar that made a person write love songs and the golden monkey that gave its owner whatever he desired. She even learned about fruit that would kill with one taste.

"If I ever go away, you must take care of the store," Mrs. Root said one afternoon.

"I will," Lena promised.

The next week when Lena came to Mrs. Root's store she wasn't behind the counter. Lena went into the back room. There were a lot of red bottles on the table. Half of them were full. The rest were empty.

Lena looked down and cried out. There was a dead man lying on the floor behind the table in a lot of blood. Mrs. Root was sitting beside him.

Lena screamed.

Mrs. Root held up a red bottle dripping with blood. The dead man's blood. "Now you know the secret ingredient," she said.

Lena was too horrified to scream again. She stumbled out of the room and ran out of the store. She thought she might be sick. *I've soaked in a dead man's blood,* she thought over and over. *All this time I've been soaking in blood.* She rested against a building, breathing hard. Her legs felt weak. *I'll never use that bath again,* she thought. *I'll never go back to that store.*

Lena still felt weak when she got home and threw herself into Rand's arms. "What's wrong?" he asked.

"I saw something terrible," Lena said.

"You're with me now," Rand said. "Everything will be all right."

Lena didn't go back to Mrs. Root's or take her bath. At first she was as beautiful as ever. Then she started to look older. Rand worked late every night and stopped kissing her goodbye in the morning. Lena wished she could take her special bath but what about the dead man?

One night Rand and Lena went to a party. Lena bought a new dress and got her hair done. But when she got to the party there was a young, pretty girl there that all the men looked at. Rand looked at her more than anyone else. He danced with the girl while Lena sat by herself. *He's going to leave me for her,* thought Lena. *He can't love me when I'm not beautiful. No one can.*

Two women stood near Lena watching Rand and the young girl dance. "He hasn't taken his eyes off her all night," one of the women said.

Lena couldn't stand it any longer. Rand should be dancing with her. The other women should be looking at her!

Lena needed her beauty bath and she was going to get it.

# Chapter 3

# Waiting for Rand

Lena went back to Mrs. Root's store and got a bottle of the special bath. She soaked in it every week and she didn't think about the dead man on the floor. She only thought about being beautiful.

"It is time for your test," said Mrs. Root one day when Lena came for more bath. "You may have your bath but you will make it yourself. You'll cut up the plants, mix them together, and make the special ingredient yourself. You must find a man, kill him, and take his blood. Then you'll have your bath."

"What?! I can't kill anyone," said Lena.

"Why not?" asked Mrs. Root. "You know what's in your bath. You already soak in a man's blood to be beautiful. You only need to learn to kill the man yourself."

"I can't," Lena said. "I can't kill anyone."

Lena went home without her bath and had dinner with Rand.

"I love you," said Rand looking at her in the candlelight.

"Would you love me even if I wasn't beautiful?" Lena asked.

"Of course," Rand said.

But soon Rand started to read the newspaper at the breakfast table and he worked late every evening. Someone called the house, and Lena was sure it was the girl from the party. If Lena called Rand at work, he never had time to talk to her.

Lena stayed in the house all day sitting in front of the mirror. She looked older and uglier every day. She wanted to be beautiful but how could she kill for it?

One morning Lena woke up feeling sad because it was her birthday. Rand didn't even remember. "I'm making a special dinner tonight," Lena told him.

"I'll come home early," Rand said, kissing her goodbye.

*Maybe he really does love me,* Lena thought. Maybe Rand would bring her flowers that night, dance with her, and make her feel like the most beautiful woman in the world because he loved her.

Lena made Rand's favorite food, cleaned the house, and set the table. She put out candles and put on a new dress. When it was almost time for Rand to come home Lena looked at herself in the mirror. She thought she looked very nice. Maybe she didn't need to be young and perfect to be beautiful.

Lena looked at the clock. Rand was late. She opened the door and looked out, but no one was coming. The dinner got cold. Lena called Rand's office, but he wasn't there. She hoped he would be home soon.

Lena waited and waited, but Rand didn't come home. It was dark outside. She knew Rand wasn't working. She called his cell phone. When Rand answered Lena heard other people talking, as if Rand was at a party. "Where are you?" Lena asked.

"Oh!" said Rand. "I forgot about dinner. I'm sorry."

"Where are you?" Lena asked again.

"I'm working," Rand said. "I won't be home until late. Don't wait up." Over the phone Lena heard a woman laughing.

"I'm really sorry about dinner," Rand said.

"I'll see you tonight," said Lena softly. She hung up the phone and washed the dishes. She took off her new dress. Rand probably wouldn't have noticed it anyway. If a woman was beautiful it didn't matter what she wore. A woman who was beautiful could have any man she wanted. Even men more handsome than Rand.

It was after midnight. Lena sat at the window. She heard a car on the road and turned out the lights. It was Rand. Lena went to the kitchen and took out a knife.

Rand got out of his car and looked at the house. The lights were off. He thought Lena was asleep. He walked up to the door and put his key in the lock. He never saw Lena crouched behind the door with a knife. She was ready and waiting for her secret ingredient.

# Review: The Perfect Wife

**A. Read each statement and circle whether it is true (T) or false (F).**

1. At the end of the story, Greg writes love songs.   T / F

2. Greg gives Mrs. Root money to pay for the perfect wife.   T / F

3. Greg's favorite flower is a lily.   T / F

4. Missy likes the same songs as Greg.   T / F

5. The fruit Mrs. Root gives Greg tastes bad.   T / F

**B. Complete each sentence with the correct word from the box.**

| bride   dreams   guitar   garden   minute   dessert   song |
| --- |

1. A woman who is getting married is called a _____ .

2. After dinner you eat _____ .

3. Greg once played music on his _____ .

4. Greg loved flowers, but he never had time to make a _____ .

5. Before he met Missy, Greg only saw his perfect wife in his _____ .

6. Missy didn't want to be away from Greg even for a _____ .

7. In the past when Greg was sad he wrote a _____ .

# Review: The Golden Monkey

**A. Choose the best answer for each question.**

1. The first thing Benny asked the golden monkey for was _____ .

   a. a new car

   b. a new jacket

   c. money

   d. eggs

**2.** Deb broke up with Benny because _____ .

    a. she loved someone else

    b. he was a thief

    c. he never called her

    d. he couldn't buy her nice things

**3.** When Benny was young, he won a prize for _____ .

    a. bowling

    b. running

    c. dancing

    d. fencing

**4.** Benny tried to get rid of the monkey by _____ .

    a. throwing it in the river

    b. giving it to Deb

    c. throwing it out the window

    d. selling it to someone else

**B.  Circle the correct word or phrase in italics to complete each sentence.**

  **1.** Benny can't afford the golden monkey, so he decides to *work for the money to buy it / steal it.*

  **2.** Benny discovers that the monkey can *grant all his wishes / answer all his questions.*

  **3.** Winning a bowling prize makes Benny feel *proud / unhappy.*

  **4.** Deb can never love Benny as long as he is *a thief / poor.*

  **5.** Mrs. Root says the monkey will leave Benny when he has no more *money / desires.*

  **6.** Benny tries to give Deb a *ring / necklace* to make her love him.

  **7.** The monkey's eyes are made of *jewels / gold.*

**51**

# Review: Beauty Secret

**A. Number these events in the order that they happened (1–7).**

_____ Lena meets Mrs. Root.

_____ Lena makes a special dinner for Rand.

_____ Lena sees her friend Lizbeth at the gym.

_____ Rand meets a pretty young girl at a party.

_____ Lena tries Mrs. Root's beauty bath.

_____ Lena finds out the secret ingredient of her beauty bath.

_____ Lena starts working for Mrs. Root.

**B. Who said this? Choose the correct answer from the box.**

| Lena | Rand | woman at the party | Mrs. Root | Lizbeth |
| --- | --- | --- | --- | --- |

1. "It's her secret so it's up to her to tell you."    _____

2. "He hasn't taken his eyes off her all night."    _____

3. "You must find a man, kill him, and take his blood."    _____

4. "I'm really sorry about dinner."    _____

5. "Would you love me even if I wasn't beautiful?"    _____

# Answer Key

**The Perfect Wife**

A: **1.** F; **2.** F; **3.** T; **4.** T; **5.** F
B: **1.** bride; **2.** dessert; **3.** guitar; **4.** garden; **5.** dreams; **6.** minute; **7.** song

**The Golden Monkey**

A: **1.** d; **2.** b; **3.** b; **4.** a
B: **1.** steal it; **2.** grant all his wishes; **3.** unhappy; **4.** a thief; **5.** desires; **6.** necklace; **7.** jewels

**Beauty Secret**

A: 2, 7, 1, 6, 3, 5, 4
B: **1.** Lizbeth; **2.** woman at the party; **3.** Mrs. Root; **4.** Rand; **5.** Lena

# Background Reading:

## Spotlight on ... *Cursed items and artifacts*

There are many myths about cursed objects. Some objects are believed to be cursed as a result of supernatural powers, like black magic or angry spirits. Other cursed objects are stolen from their rightful owners, and appear to bring misfortune to their new owners. One such cursed object is the Hope Diamond.

Today anyone can see the Hope Diamond in the Smithsonian National Museum of Natural History in Washington D.C., USA. This large blue diamond is beautiful, but it is most famous for its unusual history. A series of unfortunate events happened to several people who owned the diamond. According to legend, the Hope Diamond originally came from the eye of a stone goddess in India. In 1642, a French jeweler named Jean Baptiste Tavernier stole the diamond and brought it to France. Some say Tavernier made the goddess angry by stealing her eye and, as a result, he was later killed by wild dogs. However, others say Tavernier died an old man in France.

In the 17th century, the French king Louis XIV bought the large diamond. His grandson, Louis XVI, who also came to own it, was executed during the French revolution. Some people said that his death was the result of the diamond's curse. The diamond was stolen again in 1792 and temporarily disappeared from history. No one knew where it went.

The diamond was reportedly later bought by Thomas Hope, a member of a wealthy banking family. Although the Hope family was very rich when they bought the diamond, they later lost most of their money. Again people said it was because the diamond was cursed. The final owner of the diamond was jeweler Harry Winston, who later donated it to the Smithsonian Institution. Now people can see the Hope Diamond in the Smithsonian National Museum of Natural History without fear of the curse!

### Think About It

1. If you were able to buy the Hope Diamond, would you buy it? Why, or why not?
2. Why do you think people still wanted the Hope Diamond when people said it was cursed?

# Glossary

| | | |
|---|---|---|
| **beauty** | (*n.*) | the quality of being very attractive |
| **bowl** | (*n.*) | a deep, round object that holds food and other things |
| **bowling** | (*n.*) | a game where you try to knock down objects with a rolling ball |
| **bride** | (*n.*) | a woman who is getting married |
| **candle** | (*n.*) | a wax stick people burn to make light |
| **counter** | (*n.*) | a table or display case where things are sold in a store |
| **dessert** | (*n.*) | something sweet eaten after a meal |
| **guitar** | (*n.*) | an object with strings you play to make music |
| **gym** | (*n.*) | a place where people exercise |
| **ingredient** | (*n.*) | something that is part of a mixture, like sugar is part of a cake |
| **jar** | (*n.*) | a bottle with a wide opening |
| **magic** | (*n.*) | a strange, mysterious power that can't be explained |
| **mirror** | (*n.*) | a glass in which you can see your reflection |
| **mix** | (*v.*) | to put different things together |
| **necklace** | (*n.*) | a piece of jewelry worn around the neck |
| **prize** | (*n.*) | an object given for winning |
| **shelf/shelves** | (*n.*) | a thin, flat piece of material that holds things |
| **soak** | (*v.*) | to stay in water or something wet |
| **thief** | (*n.*) | someone who steals |
| **ugly** | (*adj.*) | unpleasant to look at |